D0484970

Mary McLeod Bethune

By Susan Evento

Consultant
Nanci R. Vargus, Ed.D.
Assistant Professor of Literacy
University of Indianapolis, Indianapolis, Indiana

Children's Press®
A Division of Scholastic Inc.
New York   Toronto   London   Auckland   Sydney
Mexico City   New Delhi   Hong Kong
Danbury, Connecticut

Designer: Herman Adler Design
Photo Researcher: Caroline Anderson
The photo on the cover shows Mary McLeod Bethune.

Library of Congress Cataloging-in-Publication Data

Evento, Susan.
  Mary McLeod Bethune / by Susan Evento.
    p. cm. – (Rookie biographies)
  Summary: An introduction to the life of Mary McLeod Bethune, an African
American educator who fought poverty and discrimination, founded a college,
and worked with Franklin Delano Roosevelt to improve opportunities for blacks.
Includes bibliographical references and index.
  ISBN 0-516-21720-8 (lib. bdg.)   0-516-25830-3 (pbk.)
  1. Bethune, Mary McLeod, 1875-1955–Juvenile literature. 2. African
Americans–Biography–Juvenile literature. 3. African American women political
activists–Biography–Juvenile literature. 4. African American women educators–
Biography–Juvenile literature. 5. African American women social reformers–
Biography–Juvenile literature. 6. African Americans–Civil rights–History–
20th century–Juvenile literature. [1. Bethune, Mary McLeod, 1875-1955.
2. Teachers. 3. African Americans–Biography. 4. Women–Biography.] I. Title.
II. Series: Rookie biography.
  E185.97.B34E98 2004
  370'.92–dc22
                              2003013684

©2004 by Scholastic Inc.
All rights reserved. Published simultaneously in Canada.
Printed in China.

CHILDREN'S PRESS, and ROOKIE BIOGRAPHIES®, and associated
logos are trademarks and or registered trademarks of Scholastic Library
Publishing. SCHOLASTIC and associated logos are trademarks and or
registered trademarks of Scholastic Inc.
16 17 18 19 20 R 20 19 18 17 16   62

Do you have a dream?

Mary McLeod Bethune did.

She dreamed of helping all
African American children
go to school.

She believed school could help
make people's lives better.

6

Bethune was born on July 10, 1875, in Mayesville, South Carolina.

Bethune's parents were slaves. They worked hard to buy a farm after slavery ended.

A church school for African American children opened when Bethune was 11. The school was a long way from the farm.

Bethune and her 16 sisters and brothers walked to school.

9

At school, Bethune studied reading, writing, and the Bible. When she was ready to go to a new school, there was nowhere to go.

African American students could not go to schools with white students.

Bethune had a chance to go
to a college away from home.
After seven years, she trained
to be a church teacher.

Bethune's first teaching job
was at her old church school.
Then she taught in Georgia and
South Carolina.

14

In 1898, Bethune married
Albertus Bethune. They had
a son and moved to Florida.

Bethune dreamed of having her
own school. She wanted a school
for African American girls.

Bethune moved to Daytona, Florida, to make her dream come true. She opened a school in 1904.

At first, there were only five students. The students paid 50 cents each week. Bethune also took students who did not have enough money to pay.

17

She worked hard to keep the school going. The school grew into a college.

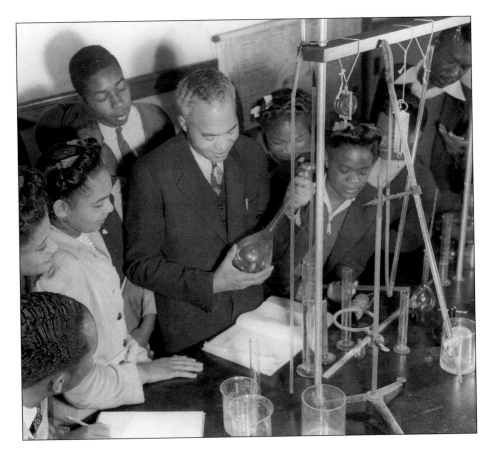

It became the Bethune-
Cookman College. Bethune
was the first president.

Bethune kept working to help make life better for all African Americans. She became famous for her work as a leader.

Four presidents of the United
States asked Bethune to work with
them. President Roosevelt made
her the leader of a special group.

This group helped African American people go to school and get jobs. Bethune was the first African American woman to have a job like this.

Bethune was the leader of many other groups, too. She also traveled around the United States.

She spoke to people about equal rights for African Americans.

Bethune lived to be 79 years old. She worked to help people live better lives. She also worked to help all people get along.

27

28

Today, a statue of Bethune stands in Washington, D.C.

It helps us remember what can happen when someone works hard to help others.

Words You Know

college

leader

president

statue

Index

About the Author

Susan Evento is a former teacher. For the past 16 years she has been a writer and editor of books and instructional materials. Recently, she was the Editorial Director of *Creative Classroom* magazine, an award-winning K–8 national teacher's magazine. Evento lives in New York city with her partner and three cats.

Photo Credits

Photographs © 2004: Corbis Images: 23 (Gordon Parks), 3 (Larry Williams); Florida State Archives: cover, 6, 14, 17, 19, 27, 28, 31 top, 31 bottom; Hulton|Archive/Getty Images: 9; Library of Congress: 10, 13, 18; National Park Service, Mary McLeod Bethune Council House, National Historic Site: 21, 30 bottom (#98), 22 (#338), 24 (#902); North Carolina State Archives: 12, 30 top; Richard Hutchings via SODA: 5.